Survey of the Academic Library Role in Course Management Systems

© 2013 Primary Research Group Inc.
ISBN: 978-1-57440-254-4
Library of Congress Control Number: 2013950023

Table of Contents

The Questionnaire

1. Does your library have one or more individuals whose primary job it is to handle the library's presence on the institutional course management system? If so describe the role of this individual or group? Do they control the presence and image of the library on the course management system? Is it done by committee? How much staff time is spent on the library's role in the course management system?

2. Does the library offer courses, seminars or otherwise provide formal training in use of the course management system to any of the following groups:
   - Students
   - Faculty
   - Library Staff

3. How does the library cover the college course management system in its information literacy training?

4. How would you describe the library's role in training instructors in how to use the college's course management system?

5. About what percentage of library staff time spent training faculty in various information technology and information literacy capabilities would you say is spent on training faculty and students in how to use the course management system?

6. How important would you say to the library's overall image are its responsibilities in training faculty and students in the use of the course management system?

7. Does the library have links to any of the following in course management systems:
   - Subject Specialists
   - Subject Specific Databases
   - Subject Specific eBooks or Books
   - Subject Specific Bibliographies

8. Has the library ever formally asked permission from instructors to edit course sites to include library links?

9. How would you describe the cooperation level of faculty in allowing librarians to add library links to their course sections on the course management system, or adding these links themselves?

10. Does your library use LibGuides?

11. Has it ever developed course specific subject guides on LibGuides?

12. In the aggregate how well used are these LibGuide course guides?

13. What is the total number of sessions recorded on Lib Guide course specific pages in a typical month while school is in session?

14. What are some of your most popular LibGuide pages or sites?

15. How many course sites are created by all instructors at your college in a given year?

16. To the best of your knowledge what percentage of these have links to library resources?

17. Are instructors in certain subject areas more likely than others to include library links in their course sites? If so which subject areas?

18. Does the library have "generic" subject guides that can be automatically linked to courses categorized by a classification system linked to the subject guides?

19. Are any of the following sets of content -- all course pages or all LibGuides or all subject guides-- searchable for instructors or students? i.e can they use search terms and search a set of course pages, or a set of LibGuides or Subject Guides?
   • LibGuides
   • Course Guides
   • Subject Guides

20. Has the library ever offered its own course through the campus course management system? If so please describe the library's experience in developing and rolling out this (these) courses.

21. Has the library course reserve system been integrated into the course management system? If so explain how you have done this.

22. Has the library ever had any issues with instructors who may abuse copyright or licensing terms by making intellectual property available over the course management system in inappropriate ways?

23. Are faculty or students able to order materials from inter-library loan through the course management system?

24. About what percentage of the faculty at your college, including both full time and adjunct faculty, would you say know how to create a link to a database, journal article or other library resource and place that link in the course pages of the course management system?

25. If your library has been able to convince instructors to create links to resources in their course management pages, or to create research guides for these pages, what have you done to be able to convince them?

26. How many of the following does your library maintain:
Subject Guides
Course Guides

27. For what percentage of the courses offered by your college does the library maintain course guides?

28. Which subject fields most commonly have library-compiled or library-assisted course guides at your college?

29. What resources - in terms of databases, websites, listservs, ezines, magazines, conferences, etc. -- has your library used to say abreast of developments in course management systems, particularly as they impact the library?

30. What advice can you offer to other academic libraries on how to better integrate library resources into course management systems?

Characteristics of the Sample

Overall sample size: 38

Broken out by Type of College
Public: 22
Private: 16

Broken out by Carnegie Class
Community College: 8
4-Year College: 9
MA/PHD Granting: 15
Research University: 6

Broken out by Full Time Enrollment
Less than 4,000: 14
4,000 – 10,000: 12
More than 10,000: 12

Broken out by Annual Tuition Cost
Less than $5,000: 13
$5,000 - $20,000: 14
More than $20,000: 11

Primary Course Management System
Angel: 6
Blackboard: 17
Canvas: 4
Desire2Learn: 6
Other: 5

Survey Participants

Arkansas Tech
Boston University
Bowie State University
Buena Vista University
Central Piedmont Community College
Coconino Community College
College of Charleston Libraries
College of Mount St Joseph
Crafton Hills Community College
Dallas Baptist University
Dixie State University
East Tennessee State University
Eastern University, Warner Library
Elmhurst College
Evans Library, Florida Tech
Forsyth Library / Ft Hays State University
Georgetown University
Gogebic Community College
Hamline University
Hope international University
Humboldt State University
Lawrence Technological University Library
Mansfield University
Mercer County Community College
Midwestern State University
Ogeechee Technical College
Penn State University
Pfeiffer University
Rasmussen College
SFCC Library
Shawnee Community College
Touro College
UMass Amherst Libraries
University of San Francisco
University of Toronto Libraries
Wellesley College Library & Technology Services
Western Michigan University
Wright State University

Summary of Main Findings

We surveyed 38 colleges: 22 of which are public and 16 are private. Eight of the colleges are community colleges, nine are 4-year colleges, fifteen are MA/PHD granting, six are research universities. Fourteen of the schools have less than 4,000 students enrolled, twelve have 4,000 to 10,000 students, and twelve have more than 10,000 students. Thirteen of the colleges have an annual tuition cost of less than $5,000, fourteen have a tuition cost of $5,000 to $20,000, and eleven have a tuition cost of more than $20,000. Six colleges use Angel as their primary course management system, seventeen use Blackboard, four use Canvas, six use Desire2Learn and five use other systems.

Staffing

We asked the participants if their library had one or more individuals whose primary job it was to handle the library's presence on the institutional course management system, and 39.47% have one or more such individuals This includes 50% of public colleges, 75% of community colleges, 58.33% of colleges with more than 10,000 students, and 53.85% of colleges with a tuition cost of less than $5,000, the highest percentages in their respective categories.

We asked the participants with one or more individuals assigned to handle the library's role in the course management system to describe the role of this individual or group, whether they controlled the presence and image of the library on the course management system, whether it was done by committee, and how much staff time is spent on the library's role in the course management system. One participant responded that the information literacy coordinator acts as a liaison between the system and library services and supports training of staff in using the building block to inset library materials into courses. Another library has an embedded librarian program coordinated by this individual, who also submits requests to the IT department for librarians to be enrolled in course shells so that they may better deliver instruction to online and in-person classes. For another library, this role is handled by several people in various departments of the library, but it is not their primary job. One library has a small committee that works with campus IT services to maintain a presence in their LMS.

Course Management And Information Literacy

We asked the participants if their libraries offered courses, seminars, or otherwise provide formal training in use of the course management system to any of the following groups: students, faculty and library staff. 18.24% of the libraries offer courses, seminars or other formal training in using the course management system for students. This includes 18.75% of private colleges, 44.44% of 4-year colleges, 21.43% of colleges with less than 4,000 students.

Formal Training in Using the Course Management System

21.05% of the libraries offer formal training to faculty in using the course management system. This includes 31.25% of private colleges, 28.57% of colleges with less than 4,000 students, 27.27% of colleges with a tuition cost of more than $20,000, and 60% of libraries who use an "other" primary course management system, the highest percentages in their respective categories.

23.68% of the libraries offer formal training in using the course management system for library staff. This includes 27.27% of public colleges, 66.67% of research universities, 50% of colleges with more than 10,000 students.,

We asked the participants how their library covers the college course management system in its information literacy training. One library offers two online certification courses that cover information and digital literacy. Another library does not have an official role in training on the course management system, but staff responds as they are able to questions students may have on the topic. One library has library related trainings and assessments using Blackboard as needed. Other libraries use library course guides, workshops, instruction sessions, online tutorials, CMS, or a one-credit hour class.

Library's Role in Training Instructors

We asked the participants how they would describe the library's role in training instructors in how to use the college's course management system. We gave respondents a choice of the following phrases to describe library policy: 1) it is virtually our exclusive responsibility, 2) it is largely our responsibility, 3) we share the task with IT, academic departments and/or others, 4) we play only a modest role, 5) we don't really play any role. 71.05% of the libraries don't really play any role. This includes 77.27% of public colleges, 75% of community colleges, 78.57% of colleges with a tuition cost of $5,000 to $20,000, and 100% of libraries who use Angel as their primary course management system, the highest percentages in their respective roles. On the other hand, it is virtually the exclusive responsibility of the libraries of 12.5% of community colleges, 14.29% of colleges with less than 4,000 students, and 20% of libraries who use an "other" primary course management systems.

We asked the participants about what percentage of library staff time spent training faculty and students in various information technology and information literacy capabilities would they say is spent on training faculty and students in how to use the course management system. The average amount of time was 8.02%. This includes 12.10% of private colleges, 14.29% of 4-year colleges, 14.65% of colleges with less than 4,000 students enrolled, and 16.15% of colleges with a tuition cost of more than $20,000, the highest percentages in their respective categories.

We asked the participants how important would they say to the library's overall image are its responsibilities in training faculty and students in the use of the course management system. 55.26% of the participants responded that their library's responsibilities were low profile and basically negligible. This includes 59.09% of public colleges, 66.67% of MA/PHD granting, 83.33% of colleges with 4,000 to 10,000 students, and 83.33% of colleges that use Angel as their primary course management system, the highest percentages in their respective categories. 40% of libraries use another system as their primary course management system, 18.18% of colleges with a tuition cost of more than 18.18% and 25% of community colleges felt their responsibilities in training faculty and students in the use of course management were important to their overall image.

Links to Course Management Systems

We asked the libraries if their libraries had links to any of the following from their course management systems: subject specialists, subject specific databases, subject specific eBooks or Books, and subject specific bibliographies. 28.95% of the libraries have links to subject specialists in their course management systems. This includes 31.82% of public colleges, 66.67% of research universities, 41.67% of colleges with more than 10,000 students, and 50% of libraries that use Angel or Blackboard as their primary course management system, the highest percentages in their respective categories.

55.26% of the libraries have links to subject specific library databases embedded in their course management systems. This includes 59.09% of public colleges, 83.33% of research universities, 66.67% of colleges with more than 10,000 students, and 75% of libraries that use Canvas as their primary course management system, the highest percentages in their respective categories.

36.84% of the libraries have links to subject specific eBooks or Books embedded in their course management system. This includes 40.91% of public colleges, 75% of community colleges, 46.15% of colleges with a tuition cost of less than $5,000, and 66.67% of libraries that use Angel as their primary course management system, the highest percentages in their respective categories.

28.95% of the libraries have links to subject specific bibliographies embedded in their course management system. This includes 31.82% of public colleges, 66.67% of research universities, 58.33% colleges with more than 10,000 students, and 35.71% of colleges with a tuition cost of $5,000 to $20,000, the highest percentages in their respective categories.

55.26% of the libraries sampled have formally asked permission from instructors to edit course sites to include library links. This includes 63.64% of public colleges, 83.33% of research universities, 75% of colleges with 4,000 students or more, and 100% of libraries that use Canvas as their primary course management system, the highest percentages in their respective categories.

Cooperation Level of Faculty

We asked the participants how they would describe the cooperation level of faculty in allowing librarians to add library links to their course sections on the course management system, or adding these links themselves. Responses ranged from excellent to not helpful.

One library answered that some faculty are very receptive while others are not. Another library has a very low adoption rate of D2L for faculty but have started using the LMS for course reserves and their circulation department is able to add content to faculty courses. One library, which has had a positive faculty response, has online courses with a librarian presence in discussions (embedded librarian), but mostly they have worked with faculty to integrate links to subject specialists, research guides, and other library resources into their course sites. One library has a library resources page automatically embedded in every BB course, but it is not subject-specific.

Use Of Libguides

71.05% of the libraries sampled use LibGuides. This includes 72.73% of public colleges, 88.89% if 4-year colleges, 83.33% of colleges with more than 10,000 students, and 100% of libraries that use Desire2Learn as their primary course management system.

65.79% of the libraries have developed course specific subject guides on LibGuides. This includes 68.18% of public colleges, 88.89% of 4-year colleges, 83.33% of colleges with more than 10,000 students, and 83.33% of libraries that use Desire2Learn as their primary course management system.

We asked the participants how well LibGuide course guides were used. Responses ranged from used very well to poorly used. One participant explained that it depended on how well the librarian promotes them in the Blackboard navigation panel, and that it's up to each individual librarian to create dynamic content related to the course assignments. Another library, whose course guides were heavily used, introduced the guides to students in a face-face instruction session delivered through IL instruction.

For the colleges in the sample, the average total number of sessions recorded on LibGuide course specific pages in a typical month while school is in session was 1,850. This includes 2,615 for public colleges, 4,685 for community colleges, 4,494 for colleges with more than 10,000 students, and 5,016 for libraries that use Desire2Learn as their primary course management system, the largest numbers in their respective categories.

Popular LibGuide Pages or Sites

We asked the participants what were some of their most popular LibGuide pages or sites ? Responses included "virtual library tour," "finding resources at the library," "what is a scholarly article?," "marketing research," and "citing business sources." Subjects included finance, nursing, art, education, English, communication studies, business, health, history, human services, literature, political science, and psychology.

Course Sites And Library Links

The average number of course sites created by all instructors at each college in a given year was 1,042.8. This includes 1,688 at public colleges, 8,000 at research universities, 8,000 at colleges with more than 10,000 students, and 2,833 at colleges with a tuition cost of less than $5,000.

Of these course sites, an average of 27.7% have links to library resources. This includes 40% of those at private colleges, 36% at 4-year colleges, 52% at colleges with less than 4,000 students, and 60% at libraries that use Canvas as their primary course management system.

We asked the participants if instructors in certain subject areas are more likely than others to include library links to their course sites and if so, which subject areas. A majority of the participants responded that certain subject areas were more prone to including library links on their course sites; these subjects included art, human services, English, communications, business, psychology, computer science, economics, political science, history, education and athletic training.

28.95% of the libraries have "generic" subject guides that can be automatically linked to courses categorized by a classification system linked to the subject guides. This includes 36.36% of public colleges, 33.33% of colleges with more than 10,000 students 38.46% of colleges with a tuition cost of less than $5,000, and 35.29% of libraries that use Blackboard as their primary course management system, the highest percentages in their respective categories.

Guides Searchable for Instructors or Students

We asked the participants if LibGuides, course guides or subject guides are searchable for instructors or students, i.e. can they use search terms and search a set of course pages or a set of LibGuides or subject guides. 47.37% of the libraries have LibGuides that are searchable for instructors or students. This includes 56.25% of private colleges, 87.5% of community colleges, 76.92% of colleges with a tuition cost of less than $5,000, and 75% of libraries that use Canvas as their primary course management system, the highest percentages in their respective categories.

21.05% of the libraries have non LibGuide course guides that are searchable for instructors and students. This includes 25% of private colleges, 50% of research universities, 41.67% of colleges with more than 10,000 students and 40% of libraries that use another system as their primary course management system, the highest percentages in their respective categories.

28.95% of the libraries have subject guides that are searchable for instructors or students. This includes 43.75% of private colleges, 50% of research universities, 41.67% of colleges with more than 10,000 students, and 54.55% of colleges with a tuition cost of more than $20,000, the highest percentages in their respective categories.

Library Courses And The Course Management System

36.84% of the libraries sampled have offered their own course through the course management system. This includes 43.75% of the libraries of private colleges, 46.67% of MA/PHD granting college libraries, 50% of colleges with 4,000 to 10,000 students, and 50% of libraries that use Desire2Learn as their primary course management system, the highest percentages in their respective categories.

Of the libraries who have offered a library science course through the course management system, we asked them to describe the library's experience in developing these courses. One library has an ANGEL course that was developed by an instruction librarian three years ago as an archive for course materials and for grading/attendance tracking, the process involving a transfer of existing material to the LMS as PDFs. The library plans to offer this course online in the near future, so it will be transferred to Canvas LMS, which works well with any device. Another library has an open-enrollment, no-credit Library Research 101 course hosted on Blackboard that is still in early stages of development but has received a positive response from instructors. One library has a librarian who transferred traditional library information courses to Blackboard, then later to Moodle when college switched to Moodle.

Course Management And Library Reserves

28.95% of the libraries have integrated their course reserve system into the course management system. This includes 31.82% of public colleges, 66.67% of research universities, 58.33% of colleges with more than 10,000 students, and 36.6% of colleges with a tuition cost of more than $20,000, the highest percentages in their respective categories.

We asked them to explain how they have done this. One participant explained that if there are reserve items submitted by an instructor, the list is linked in the default library resources page for that course. Another library is integrating course reserves through a custom widget. One library has faculty upload their own electronic reserves and directs them to the campus copy center for digitizing if necessary; several other libraries followed a similar system, supporting professors in uploading their own documents or setting links to resources within their databases. One library has done away with their electronic reserves and has all articles available on Blackboard.

Issues with Instructors Abusing Copyright or Licensing Terms

31.58% of the libraries have had issues with instructors who may abuse copyright or licensing terms by making intellectual property available over the course management system in inappropriate ways. This includes 55.56% of 4-year colleges, 41.67% of colleges with more than 10,000 students, 42.86% of colleges with a tuition cost of $5,000 to $20,000, and 41.18% of libraries that use Blackboard as their primary course management system.

We asked the participants if faculty or students were able to order materials from inter-library loan through the course management system, and 13.16% responded that they were able to do so. This includes 18.18% of libraries of public colleges, 33.33% of 4-year colleges, 21.43% of colleges with less than 4,000 students enrolled, and 50% of libraries that use Angel as their primary course management system, the highest percentages in their respective categories.

Relations With Faculty And Students

An estimated 24.75% of the faculty at the colleges in the sample know how to create a link to a database, journal article or other library resource and place that link in the course pages of the course management system. This includes 29.58% of faculty at private colleges, 29.63% at 4-year colleges, 39% at colleges with more than 10,000 students, and 32.57% of colleges with a tuition cost of more than $20,000, the highest percentages in their respective categories. These are estimates made by librarians sampled, not actual results from surveys of faculty.

We asked the participants what they have done to convince instructors to create links to resources in their course management pages or to create research guides for these pages. A majority of the responses included variations on the theme of establishing relationships with and communicating with them on a personal level through library info literacy instruction, embedded librarianship, or simply basic through basic social networking. One library offers occasional seminars or become participants in their university's blackboard instruction·team. Other libraries use strategies such as presenting at their college's annual course management training workshop, and emails and other forms of marketing.

Number of Guides Maintained by the Library

The libraries in the sample maintained an average of 57.37 subject guides. This includes 71.37 for public colleges, 189 for research universities, 133 for colleges with more than 10,000 students and 87.18 for colleges with a tuition cost of $5,000 to $20,000, the highest percentages in their respective categories.

The libraries maintained only 49.69 course guides. This includes 52.8 for private colleges, 92 for research universities, 106.29 for colleges with more than 10,000 students and 81.17 for colleges with a tuition cost of more than $20,000, the largest amounts in their respective categories.

The library maintains course guides for 7.05% of the courses offered by each college. This includes 8.63% for private colleges, 9.71% for community colleges, 22.67% for colleges with a total enrollment of more than 10,000 students, and 10.82% for libraries that use Blackboard as their primary course management system, the largest amounts in their respective categories.

We asked the participants which subject fields mostly commonly have library-compiled or library-assisted course guides at their college. Responses included history, art, social sciences, human services, English, communications, business, nursing, psychology, computer science, education, health, math, sociology, dance, and political science.

Resources

We asked the participants what resources, in terms of databases, websites, listservs, ezines, magazines, conferences, etc., has their library used to stay abreast of developments in course management systems, particularly as they impact the library. One library typically relies on their ITS and ELearning Departments to keep them updated of what goes on, as well as paying attention to presentations at state-wide conferences and analysing peer libraries around the state and region. Other services used include websites, listservs, Sakai Conference and User Group, Google Apps for education resources, LMS User groups, Educause, Chronicle of Higher Ed, Journal of Academic Librarianship, blogs, and webinars.

Advice for Other Academic Libraries

We asked the participants what advice they would offer to other academic libraries on how to better integrate library resources into course management systems. One library suggested integrating resources early in the adoption of the LMS because it's harder to get automated insertion of library materials after launch, and also to make friends with and be a very good partner with whoever runs your course management system. Another library advised starting an embedded program, especially to reach out to online students. Other suggestions included working closely with Instructional Design and Technology Staff, meeting with faculty to provide library and tech services, and seeing how other libraries have integrated library resources into their LMS and then working with their campus IT to make it happen. A majority of the participants stressed the importance of communication.

Chapter 1. Staffing

Table 1.1 Does your library have one or more individuals whose primary job it is to handle the library's presence on the institutional course management system?

	No Answer	Yes	No
Entire sample	0.00%	39.47%	60.53%

Table 1.2 Does your library have one or more individuals whose primary job it is to handle the library's presence on the institutional course management system? Broken out by Type of College

Type of College	Yes	No
Public	50.00%	50.00%
Private	25.00%	75.00%

Table 1.3 Does your library have one or more individuals whose primary job it is to handle the library's presence on the institutional course management system? Broken out by Carnegie Class

Carnegie Class	Yes	No
Community College	75.00%	25.00%
4-Year College	11.11%	88.89%
MA/PHD Granting	40.00%	60.00%
Research University	33.33%	66.67%

Table 1.4 Does your library have one or more individuals whose primary job it is to handle the library's presence on the institutional course management system? Broken out by Full Time Enrollment

Full Time Enrollment	Yes	No
Less than 4,000	35.71%	64.29%
4,000 – 10,000	25.00%	75.00%
More than 10,000	58.33%	41.67%

Table 1.5 Does your library have one or more individuals whose primary job it is to handle the library's presence on the institutional course management system? Broken out by Annual Tuition Cost

Annual Tuition Cost	Yes	No
Less than $5,000	53.85%	46.15%
$5,000 - $20,000	42.86%	57.14%
More than $20,000	18.18%	81.82%

Table 1.6 Does your library have one or more individuals whose primary job it is to handle the library's presence on the institutional course management system? Broken out by Primary Course Management System

Primary Course Management System	Yes	No
Angel	50.00%	50.00%
Blackboard	35.29%	64.71%
Canvas	50.00%	50.00%
Desire2Learn	50.00%	50.00%
Other	20.00%	80.00%

Table 1.7 If so describe the role of this individual or group? Do they control the presence and image of the library on the course management system? Is it done by committee? How much staff time is spent on the library's role in the course management system?

1. Information Literacy coordinator (me) acts as a liaison between the system and library services, supports training of staff in using the building block to insert library materials into courses. Library ITS runs the building block, troubleshoots tech problems, also supports training. Total time spent was much larger when the system was introduced (approx. 25% FTE), now it's less than 10%.

2. CPCC has an embedded librarian program. I coordinate this program and submit requests to our IT department for librarians to be enrolled in course shells so that they may better deliver instruction to online and in-person classes. In most of these courses, our role is designated as Course Builder because any higher level would allow librarians access to grades. According to our college administration, this causes a conflict of interest with FERPA - we are currently working to change this. We are also working on a special role for my position so that I can enroll librarians in courses without having submit individual request to our IT dept. Librarians spend varying amounts of time in their respective course shells - whatever it takes to deliver quality instruction. However, Blackboard our Blackboard presence is only one part of a multifaceted approach.

3. This is being handled by several people in various departments of the library, but it is not their primary job. People from the circulation and library computing departments are working on a library widget that faculty can select and a couple of people in reference are working on tutorials and assessment options but these roles are part of their other ongoing duties.

4. Our library has a small committee that works with campus IT services to maintain a presence in our LMS, which manifests as a link to the library website. Time spent is minimal.

5. There are several people involved in having a BB presence, but it is not a primary job for any of them.

6. We are working on getting a presence.

7. The director of the library is responsible for our presence on the CMS. All work is done by the director, there is no committee. The director spends about 5 hours per semester working on the CMS.

8. One is the information literacy librarian who works with individual professors to design what he/she wants. The other is our reference systems specialist who handles the technical part of creating tutorials, or any other issues related to making Angel, our LMS, work for the library's needs. These 2 work together as needed which is about 3 hours per month in the academic year.

9. We have one person who is our library liaison to the Blackboard community, adds and edits our content.

10. The library has one individual who works with the course management system admin to post information about the library. She spends about an hour a month.

11. We do not do too much on Blackboard, as there is a department in IT that controls much of it and another department that teaches how to use it.

12. Distance education services librarian - corresponds with faculty and students Reference and Course development - works with faculty on integration of library resources within the course.
13. Head, Technology Support Services. Amount of time varies, depending on upgrades, services, etc.
14. Our "off campus librarian" handles the majority of the library's presence on our CMS. She has very little direct control, but instead works with the distance learning/online learning office. This accounts for a substantial part of her job time, but not all, since she has other responsibilities related to our branch campuses and other online platforms for library materials (such as LibGuides). My best guess is that about half of her time is related to projects involving the CMS. In some cases, an ad hoc committee will be formed within the library to determine what changes should be made in the library's presence in the CMS. For example, when establishing a librarian "role" for librarians embedded in online classes, an ad hoc committee was established to determine what features of the course would be accessible to the librarian and what features would be blocked. Some other librarians are embedded in online classes, but not many, and this does not take much of their time (compared to other responsibilities).
15. The distance education librarian is embedded in courses and works with eLearning to promote the library in the CMS. Other librarians are also embedded, as needed.
16. eLearning department, which include Library Services. The department works collaboratively to develop the library's presence and role in the course management system.
17. The library has only a link to our home page in the course management system. No other level of organized integration has been authorized, but we'd love to be more integrated.
18. The person in charge is part of the learning resource center. He is part of the library staff, and takes suggestions from other library staff. He is full-time for instructional technology. Other library staff spend probably 10-15 hours an academic year.

Chapter 2. Course Management and Information Literacy

Table 2 Does the library offer courses, seminars or otherwise provide formal training in use of the course management system to any of the following groups:

Table 2.1.1 Does the library offer Courses, seminars, or any other formal training in using the course management system for Students?

	Yes	No
Entire sample	18.42%	81.58%

Table 2.1.2 Does the library offer Courses, seminars, or any other formal training in using the course management system for Students? Broken out by Type of College

Type of College	Yes	No
Public	18.18%	81.82%
Private	18.75%	81.25%

Table 2.1.3 Does the library offer Courses, seminars, or any other formal training in using the course management system for Students? Broken out by Carnegie Class

Carnegie Class	Yes	No
Community College	25.00%	75.00%
4-Year College	44.44%	55.56%
MA/PHD Granting	6.67%	93.33%
Research University	0.00%	100.00%

Table 2.1.4 Does the library offer Courses, seminars, or any other formal training in using the course management system for Students? Broken out by Full Time Enrollment

Full Time Enrollment	Yes	No
Less than 4,000	21.43%	78.57%
4,000 – 10,000	16.67%	83.33%
More than 10,000	16.67%	83.33%

Table 2.1.5 Does the library offer Courses, seminars, or any other formal training in using the course management system for Students? Broken out by Annual Tuition Cost

Annual Tuition Cost	Yes	No
Less than $5,000	15.38%	84.62%
$5,000 - $20,000	28.57%	71.43%
More than $20,000	9.09%	90.91%

Table 2.1.6 Does the library offer Courses, seminars, or any other formal training in using the course management system for Students? Broken out by Primary Course Management System

Primary Course Management System	Yes	No
Angel	16.67%	83.33%
Blackboard	17.65%	82.35%
Canvas	0.00%	100.00%
Desire2Learn	16.67%	83.33%
Other	40.00%	60.00%

Table 2.2.1 Does the library offer Courses, seminars, or any other formal training in using the course management system for Faculty?

	Yes	No
Entire sample	21.05%	78.95%

Table 2.2.2 Does the library offer Courses, seminars, or any other formal training in using the course management system for Faculty? Broken out by Type of College

Type of College	Yes	No
Public	13.64%	86.36%
Private	31.25%	68.75%

Table 2.2.3 Does the library offer Courses, seminars, or any other formal training in using the course management system for Faculty? Broken out by Carnegie Class

Carnegie Class	Yes	No
Community College	12.50%	87.50%
4-Year College	33.33%	66.67%
MA/PHD Granting	13.33%	86.67%
Research University	33.33%	66.67%

Table 2.2.4 Does the library offer Courses, seminars, or any other formal training in using the course management system for Faculty? Broken out by Full Time Enrollment

Full Time Enrollment	Yes	No
Less than 4,000	28.57%	71.43%
4,000 – 10,000	8.33%	91.67%
More than 10,000	25.00%	75.00%

Table 2.2.5 Does the library offer Courses, seminars, or any other formal training in using the course management system for Faculty? Broken out by Annual Tuition Cost

Annual Tuition Cost	Yes	No
Less than $5,000	15.38%	84.62%
$5,000 - $20,000	21.43%	78.57%
More than $20,000	27.27%	72.73%

31

Table 2.2.6 Does the library offer Courses, seminars, or any other formal training in using the course management system for Faculty? Broken out by Primary Course Management System

Primary Course Management System	Yes	No
Angel	16.67%	83.33%
Blackboard	17.65%	82.35%
Canvas	0.00%	100.00%
Desire2Learn	16.67%	83.33%
Other	60.00%	40.00%

Table 2.3.1 Does the library offer Courses, seminars, or any other formal training in using the course management system for Library Staff?

	Yes	No
Entire sample	23.68%	76.31%

Table 2.3.2 Does the library offer Courses, seminars, or any other formal training in using the course management system for Library Staff? Broken out by Type of College

Type of College	Yes	No
Public	27.27%	72.73%
Private	18.75%	81.25%

Table 2.3.3 Does the library offer Courses, seminars, or any other formal training in using the course management system for Library Staff? Broken out by Carnegie Class

Carnegie Class	Yes	No
Community College	25.00%	75.00%
4-Year College	22.22%	77.78%
MA/PHD Granting	6.67%	93.34%
Research University	66.67%	33.33%

Table 2.3.4 Does the library offer Courses, seminars, or any other formal training in using the course management system for Library Staff? Broken out by Full Time Enrollment

Full Time Enrollment	Yes	No
Less than 4,000	21.43%	78.57%
4,000 – 10,000	0.00%	100.00%
More than 10,000	50.00%	50.00%

Table 2.3.5 Does the library offer Courses, seminars, or any other formal training in using the course management system for Library Staff? Broken out by Annual Tuition Cost

Annual Tuition Cost	Yes	No
Less than $5,000	23.08%	76.92%
$5,000 - $20,000	21.43%	78.57%
More than $20,000	27.27%	72.73%

Table 2.3.6 Does the library offer Courses, seminars, or any other formal training in using the course management system for Library Staff? Broken out by Primary Course Management System

Primary Course Management System	Yes	No
Angel	16.67%	83.33%
Blackboard	23.53%	76.47%
Canvas	0.00%	100.00%
Desire2Learn	16.67%	83.33%
Other	60.00%	40.00%

Table 2.4 How does the library cover the college course management system in its information literacy training?

1. If the specific class has a need for library resources then the links are covered
2. Something I didn't mention in question 8 is that we also partner with our E-Learning Department to offer Blackboard Orientation sessions at the beginning of each semester. These are designed to help students who may have never taken an online class before get a little more comfortable using the tool. We also do library related trainings and assessments using BB, as needed, but not regularly. E-Learning educates CPCC faculty on how to best use Blackboard.
3. We have two online certification courses that cover information and digital literacy.
4. The library reference staff responds as they are able to questions students may have about the course management system while they are using it in the library, but the library does not have an official role in training on the course management system. A separate department trains faculty on the system.
5. As a merged organization (IT/Library), we have "library" staff who are both Instructional Techs and Librarians so it is difficult to parse out what the "library" does per se. However, the instructional librarians are able to access each of the course sites in Sakai and Google. They work with faculty to decide what tools to use and how to design their courses with digital literacy skills in mind. They also work with students to teach them how to navigate their course sites and resources.
6. Library Course Guides.
7. It doesn't. We have a campus Instructional Technologies team that provides training - unaffiliated with the library.
8. It is a separate, optional workshop different from library orientation and instruction sessions.
9. It provides links to the library, ask a librarian, and has an embedded librarian in a key course. We provide information on how to log in when asked.
10. We use the CMS but we don't give any training on the use itself.
11. Same as in F2F; when an instructor asks for information literacy, we provide and design it especially for that particular class.
12. Refers to it, illustrates with it.
13. Does not cover.
14. It is done independently of the library, though we do teach faculty how to create links to library resources, and it is used to authenticate users off-campus.
15. Does not, except within a library taught graduate course.
16. Online tutorials for faculty and students, workshops during the semester on how to integrate library services into LMS for faculty.
17. The library does not teach anything about using the CMS as part of information literacy instruction.
18. It doesn't currently.
19. Another division covers this.
20. It only does by instructor request.
21. Mentioned it only.
22. Part of orientation.

23. No information literacy training.
24. Depends on the liaison librarian.
25. The library is not in charge of training students how to navigate or use the university's course management system. That training is provided by the Center for Teaching and Learning. We do use the system to administer a post-instruction IL assessment quiz. The library does assist faculty who need to create links to our online materials in their Blackboard courses.
26. I use it to teach a 1 credit hour class. I am starting to become more involved with other classes by creating Tegrity presentations for specific classes and/or assignments.
27. Provides a tutorial and offers a help desk. Library staff provide hands-on help. Webinars and on-site workshops train staff and faculty.

Table 3.1 How would you describe the library's role in training instructors in how to use the college's course management system?

	It is virtually our exclusive responsibility	We share the task with IT, academic departments and/or others	We play only a modest role	We don't really play any role
Entire sample	5.26%	5.26%	18.42%	71.05%

Table 3.2 How would you describe the library's role in training instructors in how to use the college's course management system? Broken out by Type of College

Type of College	It is virtually our exclusive responsibility	We share the task with IT, academic departments and/or others	We play only a modest role	We don't really play any role
Public	4.55%	0.00%	18.18%	77.27%
Private	6.25%	12.50%	18.75%	62.50%

Table 3.3 How would you describe the library's role in training instructors in how to use the college's course management system? Broken out by Carnegie Class

Carnegie Class	It is virtually our exclusive responsibility	We share the task with IT, academic departments and/or others	We play only a modest role	We don't really play any role
Community College	12.50%	0.00%	12.50%	75.00%
4-Year College	0.00%	11.11%	22.22%	66.67%
MA/PHD Granting	6.67%	0.00%	20.00%	73.33%
Research University	0.00%	16.67%	16.67%	66.67%

Table 3.4 How would you describe the library's role in training instructors in how to use the college's course management system? Broken out by Full Time Enrollment

Full Time Enrollment	It is virtually our exclusive responsibility	We share the task with IT, academic departments and/or others	We play only a modest role	We don't really play any role
Less than 4,000	14.29%	7.14%	14.29%	64.29%
4,000 – 10,000	0.00%	0.00%	25.00%	75.00%
More than 10,000	0.00%	8.33%	16.67%	75.00%

Table 3.5 How would you describe the library's role in training instructors in how to use the college's course management system? Broken out by Annual Tuition Cost

Annual Tuition Cost	It is virtually our exclusive responsibility	We share the task with IT, academic departments and/or others	We play only a modest role	We don't really play any role
Less than $5,000	7.69%	0.00%	15.38%	76.92%
$5,000 - $20,000	0.00%	0.00%	21.43%	78.57%
More than $20,000	9.09%	18.18%	18.18%	54.55%

Table 3.6 How would you describe the library's role in training instructors in how to use the college's course management system? Broken out by Primary Course Management System

Primary Course Management System	It is virtually our exclusive responsibility	We share the task with IT, academic departments and/or others	We play only a modest role	We don't really play any role
Angel	0.00%	0.00%	0.00%	100.00%
Blackboard	5.88%	5.88%	23.53%	64.71%
Canvas	0.00%	0.00%	25.00%	75.00%
Desire2Learn	0.00%	0.00%	16.67%	83.33%
Other	20.00%	20.00%	20.00%	40.00%

Table 4.1 About what percentage of library staff time spent training faculty in various information technology and information literacy capabilities would you say is spent on training faculty and students in how to use the course management system?

	Mean	Median	Minimum	Maximum
Entire sample	8.02%	0.50%	0.00%	70.00%

Table 4.2 About what percentage of library staff time spent training faculty in various information technology and information literacy capabilities would you say is spent on training faculty and students in how to use the course management system? Broken out by Type of College

Type of College	Mean	Median	Minimum	Maximum
Public	4.62%	0.05%	0.00%	45.00%
Private	12.10%	1.00%	0.00%	70.00%

Table 4.3 About what percentage of library staff time spent training faculty in various information technology and information literacy capabilities would you say is spent on training faculty and students in how to use the course management system? Broken out by Carnegie Class

Carnegie Class	Mean	Median	Minimum	Maximum
Community College	8.71%	5.00%	0.00%	45.00%
4-Year College	14.29%	10.00%	0.00%	70.00%
MA/PHD Granting	5.11%	0.00%	0.00%	50.00%
Research University	6.75%	1.00%	0.00%	25.00%

Table 4.4 About what percentage of library staff time spent training faculty in various information technology and information literacy capabilities would you say is spent on training faculty and students in how to use the course management system? Broken out by Full Time Enrollment

Full Time Enrollment	Mean	Median	Minimum	Maximum
Less than 4,000	14.65%	5.00%	0.00%	70.00%
4,000 – 10,000	3.20%	0.50%	0.00%	10.00%
More than 10,000	4.21%	0.05%	0.00%	25.00%

Table 4.5 About what percentage of library staff time spent training faculty in various information technology and information literacy capabilities would you say is spent on training faculty and students in how to use the course management system? Broken out by Annual Tuition Cost

Annual Tuition Cost	Mean	Median	Minimum	Maximum
Less than $5,000	6.10%	0.50%	0.00%	45.00%
$5,000 - $20,000	3.24%	0.00%	0.00%	10.00%
More than $20,000	16.15%	3.00%	0.00%	70.00%

Table 4.6 About what percentage of library staff time spent training faculty in various information technology and information literacy capabilities would you say is spent on training faculty and students in how to use the course management system? Broken out by Primary Course Management System

Primary Course Management System	Mean	Median	Minimum	Maximum
Angel	2.50%	0.00%	0.00%	10.00%
Blackboard	7.38%	1.50%	0.00%	50.00%
Canvas	2.00%	1.00%	0.00%	5.00%
Desire2Learn	2.02%	0.00%	0.00%	10.00%
Other	38.50%	45.00%	0.50%	70.00%

Table 5.1 How important would you say to the library's overall image are its responsibilities in training faculty and students in the use of the course management system?

	No Answer	Important	Somewhat important	Not too important	Low profile and basically negligible
Entire sample	2.63%	10.53%	7.89%	23.68%	55.26%

Table 5.2 How important would you say to the library's overall image are its responsibilities in training faculty and students in the use of the course management system? Broken out by Type of College

Type of College	No Answer	Important	Somewhat important	Not too important	Low profile and basically negligible
Public	4.55%	9.09%	9.09%	18.18%	59.09%
Private	0.00%	12.50%	6.25%	31.25%	50.00%

Table 5.3 How important would you say to the library's overall image are its responsibilities in training faculty and students in the use of the course management system? Broken out by Carnegie Class

Carnegie Class	No Answer	Important	Somewhat important	Not too important	Low profile and basically negligible
Community College	0.00%	25.00%	12.50%	12.50%	50.00%
4-Year College	0.00%	11.11%	0.00%	44.44%	44.44%
MA/PHD Granting	6.67%	6.67%	0.00%	20.00%	66.67%
Research University	0.00%	0.00%	33.33%	16.67%	50.00%

Table 5.4 How important would you say to the library's overall image are its responsibilities in training faculty and students in the use of the course management system? Broken out by Full Time Enrollment

Full Time Enrollment	No Answer	Important	Somewhat important	Not too important	Low profile and basically negligible
Less than 4,000	0.00%	21.43%	7.14%	35.71%	35.71%
4,000 – 10,000	0.00%	0.00%	0.00%	16.67%	83.33%
More than 10,000	8.33%	8.33%	16.67%	16.67%	50.00%

Table 5.5 How important would you say to the library's overall image are its responsibilities in training faculty and students in the use of the course management system? Broken out by Annual Tuition Cost

Annual Tuition Cost	No Answer	Important	Somewhat important	Not too important	Low profile and basically negligible
Less than $5,000	0.00%	15.38%	15.38%	15.38%	53.85%
$5,000 - $20,000	7.14%	0.00%	0.00%	28.57%	64.29%
More than $20,000	0.00%	18.18%	9.09%	27.27%	45.45%

Table 5.6 How important would you say to the library's overall image are its responsibilities in training faculty and students in the use of the course management system? Broken out by Primary Course Management System

Primary Course Management System	No Answer	Important	Somewhat important	Not too important	Low profile and basically negligible
Angel	0.00%	0.00%	0.00%	16.67%	83.33%
Blackboard	0.00%	11.76%	5.88%	29.41%	52.94%
Canvas	0.00%	0.00%	25.00%	25.00%	50.00%
Desire2Learn	16.67%	0.00%	0.00%	33.33%	50.00%
Other	0.00%	40.00%	20.00%	0.00%	40.00%

Table 6 Does the library have links to any of the following in course management systems:

Table 6.1.1 Does the library have links to Subject Specialists in course management systems?

	Yes	No
Entire sample	28.95%	71.05%

Table 6.1.2 Does the library have links to Subject Specialists in course management systems? Broken out by Type of College

Type of College	Yes	No
Public	31.82%	68.18%
Private	25.00%	75.00%

Table 6.1.3 Does the library have links to Subject Specialists in course management systems? Broken out by Carnegie Class

Carnegie Class	Yes	No
Community College	25.00%	75.00%
4-Year College	44.44%	55.56%
MA/PHD Granting	6.67%	93.33%
Research University	66.67%	33.33%

Table 6.1.4 Does the library have links to Subject Specialists in course management systems? Broken out by Full Time Enrollment

Full Time Enrollment	Yes	No
Less than 4,000	21.43%	78.57%
4,000 – 10,000	25.00%	75.00%
More than 10,000	41.67%	58.33%

Table 6.1.5 Does the library have links to Subject Specialists in course management systems? Broken out by Annual Tuition Cost

Annual Tuition Cost	Yes	No
Less than $5,000	30.77%	69.23%
$5,000 - $20,000	28.57%	71.43%
More than $20,000	27.27%	72.73%

Table 6.1.6 Does the library have links to Subject Specialists in course management systems? Broken out by Primary Course Management System

Primary Course Management System	Yes	No
Angel	50.00%	50.00%
Blackboard	11.76%	88.24%
Canvas	50.00%	50.00%
Desire2Learn	33.33%	66.67%
Other	40.00%	60.00%

Table 6.2.1 Does the library have links to Subject Specific Databases in course management systems?

	Yes	No
Entire sample	55.26%	44.74%

Table 6.2.2 Does the library have links to Subject Specific Databases in course management systems? Broken out by Type of College

Type of College	Yes	No
Public	59.09%	40.91%
Private	50.00%	50.00%

Table 6.2.3 Does the library have links to Subject Specific Databases in course management systems? Broken out by Carnegie Class

Carnegie Class	Yes	No
Community College	75.00%	25.00%
4-Year College	66.67%	0.00%
MA/PHD Granting	26.67%	0.00%
Research University	83.33%	0.00%

Table 6.2.4 Does the library have links to Subject Specific Databases in course management systems? Broken out by Full Time Enrollment

Full Time Enrollment	Yes	No
Less than 4,000	50.00%	50.00%
4,000 – 10,000	50.00%	50.00%
More than 10,000	66.67%	33.33%

Table 6.2.5 Does the library have links to Subject Specific Databases in course management systems? Broken out by Annual Tuition Cost

Annual Tuition Cost	Yes	No
Less than $5,000	61.54%	38.46%
$5,000 - $20,000	57.14%	42.86%
More than $20,000	45.45%	54.55%

Table 6.2.6 Does the library have links to Subject Specific Databases in course management systems? Broken out by Primary Course Management System

Primary Course Management System	Yes	No
Angel	66.67%	33.33%
Blackboard	52.94%	47.06%
Canvas	75.00%	25.00%
Desire2Learn	50.00%	50.00%
Other	40.00%	60.00%

Table 6.3.1 Does the library have links to Subject Specific eBooks or Books in course management system?

	Yes	No
Entire sample	36.84%	63.16%

Table 6.3.2 Does the library have links to Subject Specific eBooks or Books in course management system? Broken out by Type of College

Type of College	Yes	No
Public	40.91%	59.09%
Private	31.25%	68.75%

Table 6.3.3 Does the library have links to Subject Specific eBooks or Books in course management system? Broken out by Carnegie Class

Carnegie Class	Yes	No
Community College	75.00%	25.00%
4-Year College	33.33%	66.67%
MA/PHD Granting	13.33%	86.67%
Research University	50.00%	50.00%

Table 6.3.4 Does the library have links to Subject Specific eBooks or Books in course management system? Broken out by Full Time Enrollment

Full Time Enrollment	Yes	No
Less than 4,000	42.86%	57.14%
4,000 – 10,000	25.00%	75.00%
More than 10,000	41.67%	58.33%

Table 6.3.5 Does the library have links to Subject Specific eBooks or Books in course management system? Broken out by Annual Tuition Cost

Annual Tuition Cost	Yes	No
Less than $5,000	46.15%	53.85%
$5,000 - $20,000	35.71%	64.29%
More than $20,000	27.27%	72.73%

Table 6.3.6 Does the library have links to Subject Specific eBooks or Books in course management system? Broken out by Primary Course Management System

Primary Course Management System	Yes	No
Angel	66.67%	33.33%
Blackboard	35.29%	64.71%
Canvas	50.00%	50.00%
Desire2Learn	16.67%	83.33%
Other	20.00%	80.00%

Table 6.4.1 Does the library have links to Subject Specific Bibliographies in course management system?

	Yes	No
Entire sample	28.95%	71.05%

Table 6.4.2 Does the library have links to Subject Specific Bibliographies in course management system? Broken out by Type of College

Type of College	Yes	No
Public	31.82%	68.18%
Private	25.00%	75.00%

Table 6.4.3 Does the library have links to Subject Specific Bibliographies in course management system? Broken out by Carnegie Class

Carnegie Class	Yes	No
Community College	25.00%	75.00%
4-Year College	33.33%	66.67%
MA/PHD Granting	13.33%	86.67%
Research University	66.67%	33.33%

Table 6.4.4 Does the library have links to Subject Specific Bibliographies in course management system? Broken out by Full Time Enrollment

Full Time Enrollment	Yes	No
Less than 4,000	21.43%	78.57%
4,000 – 10,000	8.33%	91.67%
More than 10,000	58.33%	41.67%

Table 6.4.5 Does the library have links to Subject Specific Bibliographies in course management system? Broken out by Annual Tuition Cost

Annual Tuition Cost	Yes	No
Less than $5,000	23.08%	76.92%
$5,000 - $20,000	35.71%	64.29%
More than $20,000	27.27%	72.73%

Table 6.4.6 Does the library have links to Subject Specific Bibliographies in course management system? Broken out by Primary Course Management System

Primary Course Management System	Yes	No
Angel	50.00%	50.00%
Blackboard	23.53%	76.47%
Canvas	0.00%	100.00%
Desire2Learn	50.00%	50.00%
Other	20.00%	80.00%

Table 7.1 Has the library ever formally asked permission from instructors to edit course sites to include library links?

	No Answer	Yes	No
Entire sample	5.26%	55.26%	39.47%

Table 7.2 Has the library ever formally asked permission from instructors to edit course sites to include library links? Broken out by Type of College

Type of College	No Answer	Yes	No
Public	9.09%	63.64%	27.27%
Private	0.00%	43.75%	56.25%

Table 7.3 Has the library ever formally asked permission from instructors to edit course sites to include library links? Broken out by Carnegie Class

Carnegie Class	No Answer	Yes	No
Community College	12.50%	37.50%	50.00%
4-Year College	11.11%	44.44%	44.44%
MA/PHD Granting	0.00%	60.00%	40.00%
Research University	0.00%	83.33%	16.67%

Table 7.4 Has the library ever formally asked permission from instructors to edit course sites to include library links? Broken out by Full Time Enrollment

Full Time Enrollment	No Answer	Yes	No
Less than 4,000	7.14%	21.43%	71.43%
4,000 – 10,000	8.33%	75.00%	16.67%
More than 10,000	0.00%	75.00%	25.00%

Table 7.5 Has the library ever formally asked permission from instructors to edit course sites to include library links? Broken out by Annual Tuition Cost

Annual Tuition Cost	No Answer	Yes	No
Less than $5,000	15.38%	53.85%	30.77%
$5,000 - $20,000	0.00%	64.29%	35.71%
More than $20,000	0.00%	45.45%	54.55%

Table 7.6 Has the library ever formally asked permission from instructors to edit course sites to include library links? Broken out by Primary Course Management System

Primary Course Management System	No Answer	Yes	No
Angel	16.67%	16.67%	66.67%
Blackboard	0.00%	58.82%	41.18%
Canvas	0.00%	100.00%	0.00%
Desire2Learn	16.67%	66.67%	16.67%
Other	0.00%	40.00%	60.00%

Table 7.7 How would you describe the cooperation level of faculty in allowing librarians to add library links to their course sections on the course management system, or adding these links themselves?

1. Good.
2. Pretty good. If we need access as Course Builders we usually get it.
3. The faculty that use our embedded program seem to appreciate it. Embedded librarians can come and go as they please, so to speak, as long as we don't change or edit content that the instructors add, we're ok.
4. Minimal cooperation.
5. At the moment, individual subject librarians ask permission to be included in the faculty member's online course as appropriate. Depending on the faculty comfort level, sometimes the librarian has faculty or TA status to post links. At other times, the librarian may be added to the course with student status so that s/he can receive e-mails through the CMS or send messages or post links to the discussion lists. At other times, faculty may add their own link to the library home page, course reserves, or a class or subject specific LibGuide, if they are aware that one exists. Once a library widget is created, faculty will have the option to add it to their course home page themselves.
6. Some have allowed librarians to add links; others do not want to allow this.
7. We have had a positive faculty response and they have been open to collaboration. We have online courses with a librarian presence in discussions (embedded librarian) but mostly we have worked with faculty to integrate links to subject specialists, research guides, and other library resources into their course sites.
8. One librarian has worked with a few faculty and it has worked really well. Had trouble generating interest from other faculty.
9. Generally cooperative.
10. We have a library resources page automatically embedded in every BB course, but it is not subject-specific.
11. We encourage faculty to provide links and have a LibGuide with instructions.
12. Not helpful.
13. Low.
14. Excellent because they ask us to do this for them.
15. We help them with links, database links, edits, uploads, etc.
16. Mostly, the faculty do this themselves with our assistance.
17. Minimal.
18. Very cooperative.
19. We have a low adoption rate of D2L by faculty. For those who use it, they are fairly willing. We have also started using the LMS for course reserves and our Circulation department is able to add content to faculty courses.
20. This has occurred only in specific courses, usually in response to a strong existing relationship between a given faculty member and a given librarian. The library has not formally requested permission from instructors AT LARGE to edit their courses, but individual librarians have asked individual faculty members and

have sometime been granted access. For those faculty who do accept librarians into their courses (and there are very few) the cooperation has been exceptional. This is likely due to the fact that once a faculty member is willing to allow a librarian into the course at all, s/he is already interested in a very collaborative relationship.

21. It depends very much on the individual. Our tutorials have been placed in many courses, however.
22. High level of cooperation.
23. They are fine with it.
24. Have not asked.
25. Non-existent.
26. Not very.
27. I can only speak from my own experience. I have been a guest and a non-editing teacher. I believe some of my colleagues have had editing access though.
28. Our faculty have opposed giving librarians direct access to their Blackboard courses. If we were responsible for teaching faculty how to use Blackboard, then we'd have a greater opportunity to have discussions about linking or embedding discipline specific library e-content into their courses.
29. Some are very receptive while others are not.
30. Cooperative. We include a link to the library's databases collection.

Chapter 3. Use of LibGuides

Table 8.1 Does your library use LibGuides?

	No Answer	Yes	No
Entire sample	0.00%	71.05%	28.95%

Table 8.2 Does your library use LibGuides? Broken out by Type of College

Type of College	Yes	No
Public	72.73%	27.27%
Private	68.75%	31.25%

Table 8.3 Does your library use LibGuides? Broken out by Carnegie Class

Carnegie Class	Yes	No
Community College	37.50%	62.50%
4-Year College	88.89%	11.11%
MA/PHD Granting	80.00%	20.00%
Research University	66.67%	33.33%

Table 8.4 Does your library use LibGuides? Broken out by Full Time Enrollment

Full Time Enrollment	Yes	No
Less than 4,000	57.14%	42.86%
4,000 – 10,000	75.00%	25.00%
More than 10,000	83.33%	16.67%

Table 8.5 Does your library use LibGuides? Broken out by Annual Tuition Cost

Annual Tuition Cost	Yes	No
Less than $5,000	69.23%	30.77%
$5,000 - $20,000	78.57%	21.43%
More than $20,000	63.64%	36.36%

Table 8.6 Does your library use LibGuides? Broken out by Primary Course Management System

Primary Course Management System	Yes	No
Angel	50.00%	50.00%
Blackboard	70.59%	29.41%
Canvas	50.00%	50.00%
Desire2Learn	100.00%	0.00%
Other	80.00%	20.00%

Table 9.1 Has it ever developed course specific subject guides on LibGuides?

	No Answer	Yes	No
Entire sample	5.26%	65.79%	28.95%

Table 9.2 Has it ever developed course specific subject guides on LibGuides? Broken out by Type of College

Type of College	No Answer	Yes	No
Public	0.00%	68.18%	31.82%
Private	12.50%	62.50%	25.00%

Table 9.3 Has it ever developed course specific subject guides on LibGuides? Broken out by Carnegie Class

Carnegie Class	No Answer	Yes	No
Community College	0.00%	37.50%	62.50%
4-Year College	11.11%	88.89%	0.00%
MA/PHD Granting	6.67%	66.67%	26.67%
Research University	0.00%	66.67%	33.33%

Table 9.4 Has it ever developed course specific subject guides on LibGuides? Broken out by Full Time Enrollment

Full Time Enrollment	No Answer	Yes	No
Less than 4,000	7.14%	57.14%	35.71%
4,000 – 10,000	8.33%	58.33%	33.33%
More than 10,000	0.00%	83.33%	16.67%

Table 9.5 Has it ever developed course specific subject guides on LibGuides? Broken out by Annual Tuition Cost

Annual Tuition Cost	No Answer	Yes	No
Less than $5,000	0.00%	61.54%	38.46%
$5,000 - $20,000	7.14%	71.43%	21.43%
More than $20,000	9.09%	63.64%	27.27%

Table 9.6 Has it ever developed course specific subject guides on LibGuides? Broken out by Primary Course Management System

Primary Course Management System	No Answer	Yes	No
Angel	16.67%	50.00%	33.33%
Blackboard	5.88%	64.71%	29.41%
Canvas	0.00%	50.00%	50.00%
Desire2Learn	0.00%	83.33%	16.67%
Other	0.00%	80.00%	20.00%

Table 9.7 In the aggregate how well used are these LibGuide course guides?

1. Used somewhat.
2. It depends on how well the librarian promotes them in the Blackboard navigation panel, the embedded course librarian posts a link that takes students to the course LibGuide. It's up to each individual librarian to create dynamic content related to the course assignments.
3. Well used.
4. Very well used.
5. Very well.
6. This coming fall term will be the first implementation of LibGuides on our campus, so we don't have any data yet.
7. Very little. We have just begun to create our guides. However, we are collaborating with faculty as we create them.
8. Modestly used.
9. Depends on the course.
10. Not too many have asked for them so it is not a major aspect of the guides.
11. Very much so.
12. Moderately.
13. Very well used compared our previous subject guides (which were barely used at all). The course-specific guides are typically created at the request of, and in collaboration with, the course instructor. This means that the instructor is much more interested in the effectiveness of the guide and in encouraging students to use it.
14. Very well-used.
15. Poorly used.
16. Not terribly well used.
17. Not very.
18. Very well.
19. They are heavily used. They are generally introduced to students in a face-to-face instruction session delivered through IL instruction within a course.
20. Well-used.

Table 10.1 What is the total number of sessions recorded on Lib Guide course specific pages in a typical month while school is in session?

	Mean	Median	Minimum	Maximum
Entire sample	1,850.62	150.00	0.00	15,000.00

Table 10.2 What is the total number of sessions recorded on Lib Guide course specific pages in a typical month while school is in session? Broken out by Type of College

Type of College	Mean	Median	Minimum	Maximum
Public	2,615.00	100.00	0.00	15,000.00
Private	627.60	200.00	3.00	2,600.00

Table 10.3 What is the total number of sessions recorded on Lib Guide course specific pages in a typical month while school is in session? Broken out by Carnegie Class

Carnegie Class	Mean	Median	Minimum	Maximum
Community College	4,685.00	4,685.00	4,685.00	4,685.00
4-Year College	277.00	50.00	10.00	1,000.00
MA/PHD Granting	3,070.60	150.00	0.00	15,000.00
Research University	1,317.50	1,317.50	35.00	2,600.00

Table 10.4 What is the total number of sessions recorded on Lib Guide course specific pages in a typical month while school is in session? Broken out by Full Time Enrollment

Full Time Enrollment	Mean	Median	Minimum	Maximum
Less than 4,000	117.67	50.00	3.00	300.00
4,000 – 10,000	247.00	25.00	0.00	1,000.00
More than 10,000	4,494.00	2,600.00	35.00	15,000.00

Table 10.5 What is the total number of sessions recorded on Lib Guide course specific pages in a typical month while school is in session? Broken out by Annual Tuition Cost

Annual Tuition Cost	Mean	Median	Minimum	Maximum
Less than $5,000	979.00	50.00	0.00	4,685.00
$5,000 - $20,000	4,081.25	650.00	25.00	15,000.00
More than $20,000	709.50	117.50	3.00	2,600.00

Table 10.6 What is the total number of sessions recorded on Lib Guide course specific pages in a typical month while school is in session? Broken out by Primary Course Management System

Primary Course Management System	Mean	Median	Minimum	Maximum
Angel	1,450.00	1,450.00	300.00	2,600.00
Blackboard	849.67	92.50	3.00	4,685.00
Canvas	10.00	10.00	10.00	10.00
Desire2Learn	5,016.67	50.00	0.00	15,000.00
Other	1,000.00	1,000.00	1,000.00	1,000.00

Table 10.7 What are some of your most popular LibGuide pages or sites?

1. For history, human services and art classes.
2. Our Citations LibGuide is by far our most popular, beyond that ones we've created for our English 111 (freshman comp equivalent) and Business 110 (Intro to Business) are among our most highly used.
3. Virtual Library Tour, Finding Resources at the Library, What is a Scholarly Article?, African Literature, Marketing Research, Research Process.
4. Medicine, Nursing, Health, Statistics, ESL, Education, Business, Citing Your Sources Patent, and Trademark Resource Center Earth & Environmental Sciences
5. Popular research guides: Citing Business Sources, Boomberg tutorial, Management as a System guide, Integrated Project Course guide.
6. General Subject Guides for History, Political Science, English, Literature; Zines.
7. Marine and Environmental Systems, HUM 1011: Fundamentals of Color 1, Copyright, Edwin A. Link, Library Basics.
8. MLA citation, Copyright guide for faculty, faculty orientation to the library.
9. Citation guides, education, nursing.
10. The guides that are taught in information literacy classes. Mostly English, psychology, and marketing.
11. APA guides, citations, writing, Refworks use.
12. Databases Alphabetical, Management, Architecture.
13. English, Communication Studies, Business, Communication Disorders, Health and Human Performance, Athletic Training.
14. OneSearch page, education, psychology, health sciences, nursing.
15. Nursing, art, education.
16. ILL and first page.
17. Finance, PR Companies.
18. RefWorks, business.

Chapter 4. Course Sites and Library Links

Table 11.1 How many course sites are created by all instructors at your college in a given year?

	Mean	Median	Minimum	Maximum
Entire sample	1,042.80	200.00	10.00	8,000.00

Table 11.2 How many course sites are created by all instructors at your college in a given year? Broken out by Type of College

Type of College	Mean	Median	Minimum	Maximum
Public	1,688.00	70.00	10.00	8,000.00
Private	397.60	200.00	65.00	900.00

Table 11.3 How many course sites are created by all instructors at your college in a given year? Broken out by Carnegie Class

Carnegie Class	Mean	Median	Minimum	Maximum
Community College	40.00	40.00	10.00	70.00
4-Year College	461.50	461.50	300.00	623.00
MA/PHD Granting	285.00	200.00	60.00	900.00
Research University	8,000.00	8,000.00	8,000.00	8,000.00

Table 11.4 How many course sites are created by all instructors at your college in a given year? Broken out by Full Time Enrollment

Full Time Enrollment	Mean	Median	Minimum	Maximum
Less than 4,000	398.60	200.00	70.00	900.00
4,000 – 10,000	108.75	62.50	10.00	300.00
More than 10,000	8,000.00	8,000.00	8,000.00	8,000.00

Table 11.5 How many course sites are created by all instructors at your college in a given year? Broken out by Annual Tuition Cost

Annual Tuition Cost	Mean	Median	Minimum	Maximum
Less than $5,000	46.67	60.00	10.00	70.00
$5,000 - $20,000	2,833.33	300.00	200.00	8,000.00
More than $20,000	447.00	411.50	65.00	900.00

Table 11.6 How many course sites are created by all instructors at your college in a given year? Broken out by Primary Course Management System

Primary Course Management System	Mean	Median	Minimum	Maximum
Angel	1,562.50	200.00	10.00	8,000.00
Blackboard	70.00	70.00	70.00	70.00
Canvas	60.00	60.00	60.00	60.00
Desire2Learn	461.50	461.50	300.00	623.00

Table 12.1 To the best of your knowledge what percentage of these have links to library resources?

	Mean	Median	Minimum	Maximum
Entire sample	27.70%	10.50%	0.00%	100.00%

Table 12.2 To the best of your knowledge what percentage of these have links to library resources? Broken out by Type of College

Type of College	Mean	Median	Minimum	Maximum
Public	15.40%	4.00%	0.00%	60.00%
Private	40.00%	20.00%	0.00%	100.00%

Table 12.3 To the best of your knowledge what percentage of these have links to library resources? Broken out by Carnegie Class

Carnegie Class	Mean	Median	Minimum	Maximum
Community College	23.67%	11.00%	0.00%	60.00%
4-Year College	36.00%	36.00%	2.00%	70.00%
MA/PHD Granting	26.80%	10.00%	0.00%	100.00%

Table 12.4 To the best of your knowledge what percentage of these have links to library resources? Broken out by Full Time Enrollment

Full Time Enrollment	Mean	Median	Minimum	Maximum
Less than 4,000	52.00%	60.00%	10.00%	100.00%
4,000 – 10,000	3.40%	2.00%	0.00%	11.00%

Table 12.5 To the best of your knowledge what percentage of these have links to library resources? Broken out by Annual Tuition Cost

Annual Tuition Cost	Mean	Median	Minimum	Maximum
Less than $5,000	18.75%	7.50%	0.00%	60.00%
$5,000 - $20,000	1.00%	1.00%	0.00%	2.00%
More than $20,000	50.00%	45.00%	10.00%	100.00%

Table 12.6 To the best of your knowledge what percentage of these have links to library resources? Broken out by Primary Course Management System

Primary Course Management System	Mean	Median	Minimum	Maximum
Angel	11.00%	11.00%	11.00%	11.00%
Blackboard	26.00%	10.00%	0.00%	100.00%
Canvas	60.00%	60.00%	60.00%	60.00%
Desire2Learn	4.00%	4.00%	4.00%	4.00%
Other	36.00%	36.00%	2.00%	70.00%

Table 12.7 Are instructors in certain subject areas more likely than others to include library links in their course sites? If so which subject areas?

1. Art, human services, social sciences.
2. Yes, English, communications, and Business are probably the most popular.
3. Yes. Psychology, computer science.
4. Yes, English, Lit, Economics, Political Science, History
5. Yes – Humanities, communications.
6. Psychology, integrated studies.
7. Yes, instructors in psychology and English.
8. Yes, English Composition.
9. No.
10. Probably College of Management is most likely to create links.
11. Communication Studies, English, Communication Disorders, Health and Human Performance, Athletic Training.
12. Yes - writing intensive/research courses, art/humanities/social sciences.
13. All courses automatically have the library link embedded.
14. No.
15. Nursing.
16. Yes, those who ask.
17. Yes; English and history and education, because they require the use of library resources in papers.

Table 13.1 Does the library have "generic" subject guides that can be automatically linked to courses categorized by a classification system linked to the subject guides?

	No Answer	Yes	No
Entire sample	7.89%	28.95%	63.16%

Table 13.2 Does the library have "generic" subject guides that can be automatically linked to courses categorized by a classification system linked to the subject guides? Broken out by Type of College

Type of College	No Answer	Yes	No
Public	9.09%	36.36%	54.55%
Private	6.25%	18.75%	75.00%

Table 13.3 Does the library have "generic" subject guides that can be automatically linked to courses categorized by a classification system linked to the subject guides? Broken out by Carnegie Class

Carnegie Class	No Answer	Yes	No
Community College	0.00%	25.00%	75.00%
4-Year College	22.22%	33.33%	44.44%
MA/PHD Granting	0.00%	26.67%	73.33%
Research University	16.67%	33.33%	50.00%

Table 13.4 Does the library have "generic" subject guides that can be automatically linked to courses categorized by a classification system linked to the subject guides? Broken out by Full Time Enrollment

Full Time Enrollment	No Answer	Yes	No
Less than 4,000	0.00%	28.57%	71.43%
4,000 – 10,000	8.33%	25.00%	66.67%
More than 10,000	16.67%	33.33%	50.00%

Table 13.5 Does the library have "generic" subject guides that can be automatically linked to courses categorized by a classification system linked to the subject guides? Broken out by Annual Tuition Cost

Annual Tuition Cost	No Answer	Yes	No
Less than $5,000	7.69%	38.46%	53.85%
$5,000 - $20,000	7.14%	35.71%	57.14%
More than $20,000	9.09%	9.09%	81.82%

Table 13.6 Does the library have "generic" subject guides that can be automatically linked to courses categorized by a classification system linked to the subject guides? Broken out by Primary Course Management System

Primary Course Management System	No Answer	Yes	No
Angel	0.00%	33.33%	66.67%
Blackboard	5.88%	35.29%	58.82%
Canvas	25.00%	25.00%	50.00%
Desire2Learn	16.67%	16.67%	66.67%
Other	0.00%	20.00%	80.00%

Table 14 Are any of the following sets of content -- all course pages or all LibGuides or all subject guides-- searchable for instructors or students? i.e can they use search terms and search a set of course pages, or a set of LibGuides or Subject Guides?

Table 14.1.1 Are LibGuides searchable for instructors or students?

	Yes	No
Entire sample	47.37%	52.63%

Table 14.1.2 Are LibGuides searchable for instructors or students? Broken out by Type of College

Type of College	Yes	No
Public	40.91%	59.09%
Private	56.25%	43.75%

Table 14.1.3 Are LibGuides searchable for instructors or students? Broken out by Carnegie Class

Carnegie Class	Yes	No
Community College	12.50%	87.50%
4-Year College	66.67%	33.33%
MA/PHD Granting	60.00%	40.00%
Research University	33.33%	66.67%

Table 14.1.4 Are LibGuides searchable for instructors or students? Broken out by Full Time Enrollment

Full Time Enrollment	Yes	No
Less than 4,000	42.86%	57.14%
4,000 – 10,000	50.00%	50.00%
More than 10,000	50.00%	50.00%

Table 14.1.5 Are LibGuides searchable for instructors or students? Broken out by Annual Tuition Cost

Annual Tuition Cost	Yes	No
Less than $5,000	23.08%	76.92%
$5,000 - $20,000	64.29%	35.71%
More than $20,000	54.55%	45.45%

Table 14.1.6 Are LibGuides searchable for instructors or students? Broken out by Primary Course Management System

Primary Course Management System	Yes	No
Angel	33.33%	66.67%
Blackboard	52.94%	47.06%
Canvas	25.00%	75.00%
Desire2Learn	50.00%	50.00%
Other	60.00%	40.00%

Table 14.2.1 Are Course Guides searchable for instructors or students?

	Yes	No
Entire sample	21.05%	78.95%

Table 14.2.2 Are Course Guides searchable for instructors or students? Broken out by Type of College

Type of College	Yes	No
Public	18.18%	81.82%
Private	25.00%	75.00%

Table 14.2.3 Are Course Guides searchable for instructors or students? Broken out by Carnegie Class

Carnegie Class	Yes	No
Community College	12.50%	87.50%
4-Year College	22.22%	77.78%
MA/PHD Granting	13.33%	86.67%
Research University	50.00%	50.00%

Table 14.2.4 Are Course Guides searchable for instructors or students? Broken out by Full Time Enrollment

Full Time Enrollment	Yes	No
Less than 4,000	14.29%	85.71%
4,000 – 10,000	8.33%	91.67%
More than 10,000	41.67%	58.33%

Table 14.2.5 Are Course Guides searchable for instructors or students? Broken out by Annual Tuition Cost

Annual Tuition Cost	Yes	No
Less than $5,000	7.69%	92.31%
$5,000 - $20,000	28.57%	71.43%
More than $20,000	27.27%	72.73%

Table 14.2.6 Are Course Guides searchable for instructors or students? Broken out by Primary Course Management System

Primary Course Management System	Yes	No
Angel	33.33%	66.67%
Blackboard	17.65%	82.35%
Canvas	0.00%	100.00%
Desire2Learn	16.67%	83.33%
Other	40.00%	60.00%

Table 14.3.1 Are Subject Guides searchable for instructors or students?

	Yes	No
Entire sample	28.95%	71.05%

Table 14.3.2 Are Subject Guides searchable for instructors or students? Broken out by Type of College

Type of College	Yes	No
Public	18.18%	81.82%
Private	43.75%	56.25%

Table 14.3.3 Are Subject Guides searchable for instructors or students? Broken out by Carnegie Class

Carnegie Class	Yes	No
Community College	12.50%	87.50%
4-Year College	22.22%	77.78%
MA/PHD Granting	33.33%	66.67%
Research University	50.00%	50.00%

Table 14.3.4 Are Subject Guides searchable for instructors or students? Broken out by Full Time Enrollment

Full Time Enrollment	Yes	No
Less than 4,000	21.43%	78.57%
4,000 – 10,000	25.00%	75.00%
More than 10,000	41.67%	58.33%

Table 14.3.5 Are Subject Guides searchable for instructors or students? Broken out by Annual Tuition Cost

Annual Tuition Cost	Yes	No
Less than $5,000	7.69%	92.31%
$5,000 - $20,000	28.57%	71.43%
More than $20,000	54.55%	45.45%

Table 14.3.6 Are Subject Guides searchable for instructors or students? Broken out by Primary Course Management System

Primary Course Management System	Yes	No
Angel	33.33%	66.67%
Blackboard	29.41%	70.59%
Canvas	25.00%	75.00%
Desire2Learn	16.67%	83.33%
Other	40.00%	60.00%

Chapter 5. Library Courses and the Course Management System

Table 15.1 Has the library ever offered its own course through the campus course management system?

	No Answer	Yes	No
Entire sample	2.63%	36.84%	60.53%

Table 15.2 Has the library ever offered its own course through the campus course management system? Broken out by Type of College

Type of College	No Answer	Yes	No
Public	0.00%	31.82%	68.18%
Private	6.25%	43.75%	50.00%

Table 15.3 Has the library ever offered its own course through the campus course management system? Broken out by Carnegie Class

Carnegie Class	No Answer	Yes	No
Community College	0.00%	12.50%	87.50%
4-Year College	0.00%	44.44%	55.56%
MA/PHD Granting	0.00%	46.67%	53.33%
Research University	16.67%	33.33%	50.00%

Table 15.4 Has the library ever offered its own course through the campus course management system? Broken out by Full Time Enrollment

Full Time Enrollment	No Answer	Yes	No
Less than 4,000	0.00%	21.43%	78.57%
4,000 – 10,000	0.00%	50.00%	50.00%
More than 10,000	8.33%	41.67%	50.00%

Table 15.5 Has the library ever offered its own course through the campus course management system? Broken out by Annual Tuition Cost

Annual Tuition Cost	No Answer	Yes	No
Less than $5,000	0.00%	30.77%	69.23%
$5,000 - $20,000	0.00%	42.86%	57.14%
More than $20,000	9.09%	36.36%	54.55%

Table 15.6 Has the library ever offered its own course through the campus course management system? Broken out by Primary Course Management System

Primary Course Management System	No Answer	Yes	No
Angel	0.00%	33.33%	66.67%
Blackboard	5.88%	35.29%	58.82%
Canvas	0.00%	25.00%	75.00%
Desire2Learn	0.00%	50.00%	50.00%
Other	0.00%	40.00%	60.00%

Table 15.7 If so please describe the library's experience in developing and rolling out this (these) courses.

1. The library teaches a face-to-face one-credit, undergrad research skills course. An ANGEL course was developed by an instruction librarian three years ago as an archive for course materials and for grading/attendance tracking. The process involved basically a transfer of existing material to the LMS as PDFs. No assignments are currently completed within the LMS. In the very near future, our course will be offered online as well, so the ANGEL course has been transferred to Canvas LMS, which works very well with any device (PC, iPad, mobile phone with any browser). The new version functions both as an archive for the face-to-face sections and a completely online course in itself. All assignments are completed within the LMS. Unfortunately, our university does not yet support Canvas (we have an authorized test version coming in spring), so all support of our course is self-managed (by me!). We link to our Canvas course from the university-supported ANGEL LMS course site.

2. We have an open-enrollment, no-credit Library Research 101 course hosted on Blackboard that is still in the early stages of development, but has been well-received by instructors, whom we are hoping will assign it in research-based courses. We also offer a 2.0 credit information literacy course that I teach, which makes use of BB.

3. Easy, well received by faculty, required for credit.

4. It was basically the syllabi for the course.

5. At the time Library was not well integrated into Blackboard and is now more integrated. In the future, we could expect to use it with more success.

6. Very stressful as it is done over and above our regular daily responsibilities

7. The library offered a small online course about a decade ago. Few students enrolled, and it was time-intensive for the instructors.

8. Low enrollment.

9. One person did it and she is now gone.

10. We are launching a one-credit, experimental library course in spring 2014

11. Lots of work developing the course itself. Blackboard use important part of the course structure and almost all readings were linked to library content.

12. We worked with our course development team; it is part of the curriculum for some of our program areas.

13. Librarian transferred traditional library information course to Blackboard, then later to Moodle when college switched to Moodle. Online course allows more use of web-based tutorials. Transition was smooth and bumps were minimal.

Chapter 6. Course Management and Library Reserves

Table 16.1 Has the library course reserve system been integrated into the course management system?

	No Answer	Yes	No
Entire sample	5.26%	28.95%	65.79%

Table 16.2 Has the library course reserve system been integrated into the course management system? Broken out by Type of College

Type of College	No Answer	Yes	No
Public	4.55%	31.82%	63.64%
Private	6.25%	25.00%	68.75%

Table 16.3 Has the library course reserve system been integrated into the course management system? Broken out by Carnegie Class

Carnegie Class	No Answer	Yes	No
Community College	12.50%	12.50%	75.00%
4-Year College	0.00%	22.22%	77.78%
MA/PHD Granting	0.00%	26.67%	73.33%
Research University	16.67%	66.67%	16.67%

Table 16.4 Has the library course reserve system been integrated into the course management system? Broken out by Full Time Enrollment

Full Time Enrollment	No Answer	Yes	No
Less than 4,000	0.00%	21.43%	78.57%
4,000 – 10,000	8.33%	8.33%	83.33%
More than 10,000	8.33%	58.33%	33.33%

Table 16.5 Has the library course reserve system been integrated into the course management system? Broken out by Annual Tuition Cost

Annual Tuition Cost	No Answer	Yes	No
Less than $5,000	7.69%	15.38%	76.92%
$5,000 - $20,000	0.00%	35.71%	64.29%
More than $20,000	9.09%	36.36%	54.55%

Table 16.6 Has the library course reserve system been integrated into the course management system? Broken out by Primary Course Management System

Primary Course Management System	No Answer	Yes	No
Angel	16.67%	16.67%	66.67%
Blackboard	5.88%	17.65%	76.47%
Canvas	0.00%	50.00%	50.00%
Desire2Learn	0.00%	50.00%	50.00%
Other	0.00%	40.00%	60.00%

Table 16.7 If so explain how you have done this.

1. If there are reserve items that have been submitted by an instructor, the list is linked in the default library resources page for that course.
2. Not yet, but it is in process right now. It is apparently being done through a custom widget. The same goes for item #32.
3. We have faculty upload their own electronic reserves and direct them to the campus copy center for digitizing if necessary (they will explain copyright restrictions at that point. We also point faculty to a webpage where we explain fair use principles.) We have a streaming video system that is integrated into our course sites to allow for video course reserves.
4. We don't provide digital eReserves anymore but support professors in uploading their own documents or setting links to resources within our databases.
5. Related, and overlapping. Faculty (or we) upload and link requests. However, books and some links are searchable on the library reserves section. So faculty can either add content, have links, or link to library reserves. Library reserves have been fading during the last years. (Except for print books)
6. Links to e-reserves are there as well as reading lists that list print reserves
7. Course reserves are linked in the library resources "box" of information that is automatically added to all online courses. Instructors can also choose to link to their specific resources in course reserves.
8. As of this fall, faculty will enroll the library as a teaching assistant in their courses and the library staff member will upload library materials to the course site.
9. We will provide customized links to reserve content and also instructions for faculty on how to do it themselves. We link to streamed/digitized films mostly, as well as some journal articles (we search to see if we already have it in our collection).
10. We did away with our electronic reserves. All articles are now available via Blackboard.
11. Though Reserves department in Access Services.

Table 17.1 Has the library ever had any issues with instructors who may abuse copyright or licensing terms by making intellectual property available over the course management system in inappropriate ways?

	No Answer	Yes	No
Entire sample	13.16%	31.58%	55.26%

Table 17.2 Has the library ever had any issues with instructors who may abuse copyright or licensing terms by making intellectual property available over the course management system in inappropriate ways? Broken out by Type of College

Type of College	No Answer	Yes	No
Public	13.64%	31.82%	54.55%
Private	12.50%	31.25%	56.25%

Table 17.3 Has the library ever had any issues with instructors who may abuse copyright or licensing terms by making intellectual property available over the course management system in inappropriate ways? Broken out by Carnegie Class

Carnegie Class	No Answer	Yes	No
Community College	0.00%	0.00%	100.00%
4-Year College	11.11%	55.56%	33.33%
MA/PHD Granting	13.33%	26.67%	60.00%
Research University	33.33%	50.00%	16.67%

Table 17.4 Has the library ever had any issues with instructors who may abuse copyright or licensing terms by making intellectual property available over the course management system in inappropriate ways? Broken out by Full Time Enrollment

Full Time Enrollment	No Answer	Yes	No
Less than 4,000	0.00%	21.43%	78.57%
4,000 – 10,000	16.67%	33.33%	50.00%
More than 10,000	25.00%	41.67%	33.33%

Table 17.5 Has the library ever had any issues with instructors who may abuse copyright or licensing terms by making intellectual property available over the course management system in inappropriate ways? Broken out by Annual Tuition Cost

Annual Tuition Cost	No Answer	Yes	No
Less than $5,000	15.38%	15.38%	69.23%
$5,000 - $20,000	14.29%	42.86%	42.86%
More than $20,000	9.09%	36.36%	54.55%

Table 17.6 Has the library ever had any issues with instructors who may abuse copyright or licensing terms by making intellectual property available over the course management system in inappropriate ways? Broken out by Primary Course Management System

Primary Course Management System	No Answer	Yes	No
Angel	0.00%	16.67%	83.33%
Blackboard	17.65%	41.18%	41.18%
Canvas	0.00%	25.00%	75.00%
Desire2Learn	16.67%	16.67%	66.67%
Other	20.00%	40.00%	40.00%

Table 18.1 Are faculty or students able to order materials from inter-library loan through the course management system?

	No Answer	Yes	No
Entire sample	7.89%	13.16%	78.95%

Table 18.2 Are faculty or students able to order materials from inter-library loan through the course management system? Broken out by Type of College

Type of College	No Answer	Yes	No
Public	4.55%	18.18%	77.27%
Private	12.50%	6.25%	81.25%

Table 18.3 Are faculty or students able to order materials from inter-library loan through the course management system? Broken out by Carnegie Class

Carnegie Class	No Answer	Yes	No
Community College	0.00%	25.00%	75.00%
4-Year College	11.11%	33.33%	55.56%
MA/PHD Granting	0.00%	0.00%	100.00%
Research University	33.33%	0.00%	66.67%

Table 18.4 Are faculty or students able to order materials from inter-library loan through the course management system? Broken out by Full Time Enrollment

Full Time Enrollment	No Answer	Yes	No
Less than 4,000	0.00%	21.43%	78.57%
4,000 – 10,000	0.00%	16.67%	83.33%
More than 10,000	25.00%	0.00%	75.00%

Table 18.5 Are faculty or students able to order materials from inter-library loan through the course management system? Broken out by Annual Tuition Cost

Annual Tuition Cost	No Answer	Yes	No
Less than $5,000	0.00%	23.08%	76.92%
$5,000 - $20,000	7.14%	14.29%	78.57%
More than $20,000	18.18%	0.00%	81.82%

Table 18.6 Are faculty or students able to order materials from inter-library loan through the course management system? Broken out by Primary Course Management System

Primary Course Management System	No Answer	Yes	No
Angel	0.00%	50.00%	50.00%
Blackboard	11.76%	0.00%	88.24%
Canvas	0.00%	0.00%	100.00%
Desire2Learn	16.67%	16.67%	66.67%
Other	0.00%	20.00%	80.00%

Chapter 7. Relations with Faculty and Students

Table 19.1 About what percentage of the faculty at your college, including both full time and adjunct faculty, would you say know how to create a link to a database, journal article or other library resource and place that link in the course pages of the course management system?

	Mean	Median	Minimum	Maximum
Entire sample	24.75%	15.00%	0.00%	70.00%

Table 19.2 About what percentage of the faculty at your college, including both full time and adjunct faculty, would you say know how to create a link to a database, journal article or other library resource and place that link in the course pages of the course management system? Broken out by Type of College

Type of College	Mean	Median	Minimum	Maximum
Public	21.13%	12.50%	0.00%	70.00%
Private	29.58%	29.00%	1.00%	65.00%

Table 19.3 About what percentage of the faculty at your college, including both full time and adjunct faculty, would you say know how to create a link to a database, journal article or other library resource and place that link in the course pages of the course management system? Broken out by Carnegie Class

Carnegie Class	Mean	Median	Minimum	Maximum
Community College	21.00%	12.50%	1.00%	70.00%
4-Year College	29.63%	32.50%	2.00%	50.00%
MA/PHD Granting	23.46%	10.00%	0.00%	65.00%
Research University	25.00%	25.00%	25.00%	25.00%

Table 19.4 About what percentage of the faculty at your college, including both full time and adjunct faculty, would you say know how to create a link to a database, journal article or other library resource and place that link in the course pages of the course management system? Broken out by Full Time Enrollment

Full Time Enrollment	Mean	Median	Minimum	Maximum
Less than 4,000	31.23%	25.00%	1.00%	65.00%
4,000 – 10,000	9.20%	10.00%	0.00%	33.00%
More than 10,000	39.00%	40.00%	10.00%	70.00%

Table 19.5 About what percentage of the faculty at your college, including both full time and adjunct faculty, would you say know how to create a link to a database, journal article or other library resource and place that link in the course pages of the course management system? Broken out by Annual Tuition Cost

Annual Tuition Cost	Mean	Median	Minimum	Maximum
Less than $5,000	20.73%	10.00%	0.00%	70.00%
$5,000 - $20,000	23.70%	12.50%	1.00%	65.00%
More than $20,000	32.57%	33.00%	10.00%	60.00%

Table 19.6 About what percentage of the faculty at your college, including both full time and adjunct faculty, would you say know how to create a link to a database, journal article or other library resource and place that link in the course pages of the course management system? Broken out by Primary Course Management System

Primary Course Management System	Mean	Median	Minimum	Maximum
Angel	19.00%	12.50%	1.00%	50.00%
Blackboard	25.36%	20.00%	1.00%	70.00%
Canvas	6.00%	6.00%	2.00%	10.00%
Desire2Learn	27.50%	30.00%	0.00%	50.00%
Other	35.00%	35.00%	10.00%	60.00%

Table 19.7 If your library has been able to convince instructors to create links to resources in their course management pages, or to create research guides for these pages, what have you done to be able to convince them?

1. Establish personal relationships or demonstrate student need.
2. Occasional seminars or participation alongside our university's blackboard instruction team.
3. We usually use library instruction or embedded librarianship to develop relationships with instructors.
4. Librarians present at the course management training workshop that is held each fall. This is our opportunity to show instructors how librarians and library resources can be part of their courses.
5. Again, so far, this has been done by individual subject librarians talking to their faculty for the most part.
6. We have offered instruction sessions to help them set up their sites and mentioned the library link at those sessions. We have also used our relationships with others in the department to advocate for our presence in online course sites.
7. There has been no formal attempt to encourage faculty to link to library resources in general, though individual library information advocates have developed LibGuides that instructors link to from their courses. This has happened as a result of conversations with instructors who have requested library instruction for their students, and in one case, as a result of a library requirement in an introduction to online learning course.
8. By not doing it for them.
9. Shown them how easy it is.
10. Not much; we're still trying.
11. We meet with all new faculty and do emphasize this whenever we are with any faculty, both in person or in groups.
12. Talked with them.
13. Individual networking, emails, marketing.
14. Mostly it is the faculty who are comfortable with the technology, and don't want to wait for someone else to do it for them. Usually we give them a brief tutorial and make ourselves available for questions.
15. We have not had to convince them. They see that it makes sense.
16. One-on-one and group instruction.
17. Ask them.
18. Talking with them works best.
19. We create the guides and work with them on the content.
20. Met with the creator of our "College" intro course about making some presentations for her Blackboard. We are on the same wavelength. No convincing, just informing. She was all for it. Most are once they understand.

Table 20 How many of the following does your library maintain:

Table 20.1.1 How many Subject Guides does your library maintain?

	Mean	Median	Minimum	Maximum
Entire sample	57.37	30.00	0.00	500.00

Table 20.1.2 How many Subject Guides does your library maintain? Broken out by Type of College

Type of College	Mean	Median	Minimum	Maximum
Public	71.37	43.00	0.00	500.00
Private	33.18	30.00	0.00	65.00

Table 20.1.3 How many Subject Guides does your library maintain? Broken out by Carnegie Class

Carnegie Class	Mean	Median	Minimum	Maximum
Community College	25.83	10.00	0.00	100.00
4-Year College	47.00	50.00	8.00	107.00
MA/PHD Granting	37.00	25.00	0.00	126.00
Research University	189.00	103.00	50.00	500.00

Table 20.1.4 How many Subject Guides does your library maintain? Broken out by Full Time Enrollment

Full Time Enrollment	Mean	Median	Minimum	Maximum
Less than 4,000	27.42	27.50	0.00	65.00
4,000 – 10,000	21.44	15.00	0.00	53.00
More than 10,000	133.22	100.00	43.00	500.00

Table 20.1.5 How many Subject Guides does your library maintain? Broken out by Annual Tuition Cost

Annual Tuition Cost	Mean	Median	Minimum	Maximum
Less than $5,000	42.83	20.00	0.00	150.00
$5,000 - $20,000	87.18	50.00	10.00	500.00
More than $20,000	35.43	30.00	0.00	59.00

Table 20.1.6 How many Subject Guides does your library maintain? Broken out by Primary Course Management System

Primary Course Management System	Mean	Median	Minimum	Maximum
Angel	36.20	30.00	15.00	56.00
Blackboard	74.69	25.00	0.00	500.00
Canvas	6.50	6.50	5.00	8.00
Desire2Learn	53.40	50.00	0.00	107.00
Other	57.80	50.00	0.00	150.00

Table 20.2.1 How many Course Guides does your library maintain?

	Mean	Median	Minimum	Maximum
Entire sample	49.69	10.00	0.00	350.00

Table 20.2.2 How many Course Guides does your library maintain? Broken out by Type of College

Type of College	Mean	Median	Minimum	Maximum
Public	47.75	10.00	0.00	238.00
Private	52.80	16.00	0.00	350.00

Table 20.2.3 How many Course Guides does your library maintain? Broken out by Carnegie Class

Carnegie Class	Mean	Median	Minimum	Maximum
Community College	33.40	4.00	0.00	150.00
4-Year College	12.57	10.00	2.00	23.00
MA/PHD Granting	69.18	6.00	0.00	350.00
Research University	92.00	100.00	26.00	150.00

Table 20.2.4 How many Course Guides does your library maintain? Broken out by Full Time Enrollment

Full Time Enrollment	Mean	Median	Minimum	Maximum
Less than 4,000	39.45	10.00	0.00	350.00
4,000 – 10,000	14.25	4.50	0.00	86.00
More than 10,000	106.29	100.00	23.00	238.00

Table 20.2.5 How many Course Guides does your library maintain? Broken out by Annual Tuition Cost

Annual Tuition Cost	Mean	Median	Minimum	Maximum
Less than $5,000	33.00	3.50	0.00	150.00
$5,000 - $20,000	47.50	17.50	0.00	238.00
More than $20,000	81.17	21.50	3.00	350.00

Table 20.2.6 How many Course Guides does your library maintain? Broken out by Primary Course Management System

Primary Course Management System	Mean	Median	Minimum	Maximum
Angel	31.80	20.00	3.00	100.00
Blackboard	68.56	6.00	0.00	350.00
Canvas	3.00	3.00	2.00	4.00
Desire2Learn	65.60	23.00	0.00	238.00
Other	36.40	10.00	0.00	150.00

Table 21.1 For what percentage of the courses offered by your college does the library maintain course guides?

	Mean	Median	Minimum	Maximum
Entire sample	7.05%	2.50%	0.00%	60.00%

Table 21.2 For what percentage of the courses offered by your college does the library maintain course guides? Broken out by Type of College

Type of College	Mean	Median	Minimum	Maximum
Public	6.14%	1.50%	0.00%	60.00%
Private	8.63%	4.00%	0.00%	25.00%

Table 21.3 For what percentage of the courses offered by your college does the library maintain course guides? Broken out by Carnegie Class

Carnegie Class	Mean	Median	Minimum	Maximum
Community College	9.71%	1.00%	0.00%	60.00%
4-Year College	6.00%	4.00%	1.00%	15.00%
MA/PHD Granting	5.80%	2.00%	0.00%	25.00%
Research University	5.00%	5.00%	5.00%	5.00%

Table 21.4 For what percentage of the courses offered by your college does the library maintain course guides? Broken out by Full Time Enrollment

Full Time Enrollment	Mean	Median	Minimum	Maximum
Less than 4,000	5.08%	2.50%	0.00%	25.00%
4,000 – 10,000	3.71%	1.00%	0.00%	20.00%
More than 10,000	22.67%	5.00%	3.00%	60.00%

Table 21.5 For what percentage of the courses offered by your college does the library maintain course guides? Broken out by Annual Tuition Cost

Annual Tuition Cost	Mean	Median	Minimum	Maximum
Less than $5,000	7.50%	1.00%	0.00%	60.00%
$5,000 - $20,000	4.43%	3.00%	0.00%	15.00%
More than $20,000	9.80%	3.00%	0.00%	25.00%

Table 21.6 For what percentage of the courses offered by your college does the library maintain course guides? Broken out by Primary Course Management System

Primary Course Management System	Mean	Median	Minimum	Maximum
Angel	7.00%	5.00%	1.00%	15.00%
Blackboard	10.82%	3.00%	0.00%	60.00%
Canvas	1.50%	1.50%	1.00%	2.00%
Desire2Learn	2.67%	3.00%	0.00%	5.00%
Other	1.33%	1.00%	0.00%	3.00%

Table 21.7 Which subject fields most commonly have library-compiled or library-assisted course guides at your college?

1. History, art, social sciences, human services.
2. English, communications, business, nursing.
3. Psychology, computer science, education.
4. Business, English composition, health sciences, science, math, and sociology.
5. Writing, English, Political Science/IR, History, communications.
6. Psychology, business, education, ministry.
7. Communication, psychology.
8. Medical related.
9. English composition.
10. Writing, nursing courses, health course, dance.
11. First Year Experience.
12. Management, Leadership, Architecture.
13. Nursing, Communication Studies, English, Business, Health and Human Performance, Athletic Training, Communication Disorders.
14. History, Political Science, English.
15. Humanities, social sciences and health science fields.
16. Nursing/Allied Health, English.
17. Education, art, nursing.
18. Psychology, English, education.
19. First Year Seminars and English 1110 (first year writing).
20. Medical and Business.
21. History, education, sciences, math, art, music, English.

Chapter 8. Resources and Advice

Table 21.8 What resources - in terms of databases, websites, listservs, ezines, magazines, conferences, etc. -- has your library used to say abreast of developments in course management systems, particularly as they impact the library?

1. We typically rely on our ITS and ELearning Departments to keep us abreast of what goes on though we do try to pay attention to presentations at statewide conferences and talk to our friend libraries around the state and region.
2. Websites, Listservs, conferences.
3. EMLIBS Listserv, attend CMS specific training offered at our institution (not library-directed), various articles on distance learning (including methods, assessment, and collaboration with faculty.
4. Sakai Conference and User Group; Google Apps for Education resources; LMS User groups.
5. Educause, Chronicle of Higher Ed, CR&L, Journal of Academic Librarianship
6. Databases, blogs, listservs.
7. Conferences and webinars, readings.
8. Listservs, conferences.
9. Mainly websites and conferences.
10. In-house training by our virtual college staff.
11. Email, online magazine links, personal contact with other academic departments
12. Journals, conferences.
13. Databases, listservs, conferences.
14. Individual librarians use different resources. I personally use listservs, conferences, and journals as my primary sources.
15. EDUCAUSE, Canvas users group, Chronicle of Higher Ed Wired News, Sloan Consortium.
16. Our instructional designers on campus.
17. Reading the professional literature, attending ACRL.
18. RSS feeds webinars.
19. Our Instruction Librarian.
20. Databases.
21. Mostly from our own IT people on campus. Then also websites, listservs, ezines, magazines, conferences.
22. library literature, ILI-L, ALA conference.
23. ACRL-IL listserv, Library 2.0, ACRL website, Information Literacy Project.
24. Library blogs.
25. Listservs, mostly; some databases and cooperative consortia creations.

Table 21.9 What advice can you offer to other academic libraries on how to better integrate library resources into course management systems?

1. Do it early in the adoption of the LMS. It's harder to get automated insertion of library materials after launch. Make friends with and be a very good partner with whoever runs your course management system.
2. Try starting an embedded program - especially to reach out to online students.
3. Work closely with Instructional Design and Technology Staff (as a team if possible) and meet with faculty to provide library and tech services you can offer them.
4. I think a good idea for others to take a look at how other libraries have integrated library resources into their universities' LMSs, and then work with their campus IT to make it happen.
5. Work with the department of learning technology or whoever manages the learning management system.
6. Talk with faculty. Communication is key. That is how we are approaching this situation and we hope it works.
7. Work closely with your online department staff and hire very patient library staff.
8. This is a problem, and I can give no advice. It helps that we chose Blackboard authentication for our proxy login for off-campus databases/full-text. Everyone has to use Blackboard to get access to these resources, so it keeps BlackBoard in everyone's view.
9. This is a time consuming duty, but very worthwhile and very helpful for distance students.
10. Work from both ends - try to coordinate with individual faculty teaching in the CMS, and also try to work with the administrators of the CMS to incorporate library information in the default setup of online courses.
11. Create formal relationships and partnerships with ITS and eLearning departments.
12. Work with instructional designers on campus.
13. the more actively you can work with faculty, the more likely they are to want to integrate library resources in the CMS
14. Just ask.
15. You are "out of the loop" if you are not involved.
16. Keep talking it up. Be ready with examples how this is effective.
17. Love to hear how others have gotten past faculty concern about access to their courses.
18. Work with your course design and development team.
19. Talk to people, go see them.
20. Talk to the faculty and get connections there. Offer some ideas and ask how you can save faculty and student time by having these resources for direction.
21. Only do it when you have the staff, time and budget. As we don't have enough staff, time or money, we don't do it.